The Adventures of Online Dating with Lolo

Lisa "LJ' Crawford

Edited by Shavonna Bush – Bush Legacy Publishing
Illustrations by Allen Howard

Printed in the United States of America

First Printing, 2021
ISBN 978-1-941749-98-2
4-P Publishing
Chattanooga, TN 3741

Contact LJ

 www.lisajcrawford.com

 ljthespeaker@gmail.com

Books by LJ Crawford

Available on Amazon

- The Master Relationship Builder Relationship Building Through the Eyes of the Employee
- Silent Screams Releasing Life's Experiences Through the Healing Power Of The Written Word
- Silent Screams Journal
- It Starts with Me
- Voices from the Edge

Available at www.lisajcrawford.com

- Speaking my Truth
- You are Enough

Contents

FOREWORD 7

INTRODUCTION 9

THE BIRTH OF LOLO 10

THE FANTASY MAKER 14

A MESSAGE FROM LOLO 16

THE HOLY ROLLER 17

THE WIDOWER 21

A MESSAGE FROM LOLO 27

THE TRICKSTER 28

YOU ARE A LUCKY WOMAN 35

MESSAGE FROM LOLO 43

EXCHANGE OF ETHNICITY OR CONFUSED 44

YOU REMIND ME OF 49

SEXY PHOTO 53

MESSAGE FROM LOLO 55

ABANDONED 56

MESSAGE FROM LOLO 78

SUGAR MOMMA- NEGATIVE 79

THE RESOURCE 81

BEWARE 83

SUCCESS STORY 87

MESSAGE FROM LOLO 93

ABOUT THE AUTHOR 97

Foreword

What can I say? 2020 found many of us stuck in homes, dreading to go outside to meet new people and casually mingle. However, there was still the need for social interaction. People began looking for more health-conscious ways of connecting with others—Que, social media dating sites.

In 2007, I met my now husband of eleven years on Black Planet.com. We dated for two and half years before he proposed on Christmas Day, 2009. Five months later, we were saying, "I do" in front of God, our family, and friends. The rest is history! We have a beautiful family and an amazing marriage.

In this hilarious telling of the quest for love, Lisa Crawford captures the highs and lows of online dating. A seasoned author, Lisa has written several books and lends her voice to many charitable causes.

Adventures of Online Dating with Lolo is sure to make you laugh and cringe alike. Now, swipe left, and enjoy!

Shavonna Bush
Bush Legacy Publishing

Introduction

Online dating is like a jungle of many different people, emotions, and personalities. It's all about what you want, what you think you want, what you hope to find, and the hope that the right one finds you.

My experience in online dating began after I raised my children. My son said, "Mom, I think you need to get online and meet someone." In other words, we don't need you hovering over us anymore.

I guess it would be okay. One of my friends was on Black People Meet, so I'll try that one. Another friend was on Plenty of Fish, so I looked around on that one, too. Someone else said I should try Match.com. I ended up being on all of them except Tinder, and that's because I am old and seasoned.

Are you ready for an adventure? Let's go!

The Birth of Lolo

The birth of Lolo came after I met Rodney on Plenty of Fish, better known as POF. When I first saw him, I thought he looked like a bunch of fun. I did not message him because I was trying to chitchat with someone else. When the chitter-chatter did not work out, he messaged me the same day. We chatted from the site for one day, and then we exchanged numbers. We started texting. He was hilarious. He always said something funny at the end of our conversation. We were off to a great start.

We were set to go out on Wednesday, but I had a meeting to attend before the date. I left work, went to the meeting, and then went straight to the agreed date location, Panera Bread. We recognized each other right away and hugged. Gee whiz, he smelled good. We sat outside.

"Hey, why did we come to Panera Bread?" He asked.

"I just thought it was cool (it was my safe place because I was there so much during the week)."

"Are you hungry?"

"I could eat," I replied.

"Will you get in my car? We can go across the parking lot to Chili's. If I get out of line with you, your car is right here, and you can escape," he said jokingly.

He helped me into the car and went across the parking lot to Chili's. We ordered appetizers and a drink. My day had been so crazy until that point. Rodney was fun. He made me laugh, and I was extremely comfortable around him. We stayed there for almost three hours. It was nice.

As promised, he took me right back to my car, hugged me, and sent me on my way. He texted to make sure I got home and said goodnight. Over the next few days, we chatted via text to set up another date. I think we had sushi and drinks. It was a great night. This went on for about five dates.

We realized that we both liked the show "Empire," so that date was at his house. I decided to hang out with him a bit longer than usual. I had worked all day and did not get a chance to go home. When he greeted me with a hug, I got lost in his cologne. Rodney always looked so nice, even in his comfortable clothes. Okay, I drifted for a moment. I'm back.

He had to run to the store, so I asked if I could take a shower while he was gone.

"Sure, Lolo, no problem."

He disappeared for a minute.

"Come on back."

He motioned for me to follow him.

Did I mention he had a lovely and comfortable home? He laid out the towel and clothes and left. I must have felt extremely safe because I took my shower and put on my yoga pants, long-sleeved t-shirt, and socks. When I ventured back into the living room, he had made me a drink and sat it on the table. He put the television on an

"Empire" episode, and I sat there and just breathed a sigh of yes!

When he got back, it was time for the show. He brought Chinese food, and we ate and watched Empire. Afterward, we chatted for a bit and decided to listen to some music.

I noticed Rodney looking at me.

"What's wrong?" I asked.

He said, "Lolo, I enjoy the time we spend together, but I have a problem with you."

"Really? What is that?"

"When we set up a date, I come home from work, and I prepare to meet you because you matter to me."

Confused, I asked, "Do I look bad or something?"

"No, but you don't prepare for me. You have been dealing with people all day, and you are tense and just not mentally ready for a date."

I thought about it. The guy I dated before him lived out of town, so I was not coming from work or a meeting when I saw him. I was prepared to see him.

"Hmmm, I will take heed of this and make some changes."

He smiled and said, "Thank you."

"Now, I have something to ask you."

"Sure, what's up?" he replied with a curious look on his face.

"Rodney, why do you call me Lolo?"

"That's your name, right?" he asked, confused.

"No! My name is Lisa."

He started jumping around.

"Wait, when we are texting, you always end your last text LOLO."

I burst out laughing.

I said, "I always type LOL because you are so funny, but my phone adds another O."

I could not quit laughing.

He said, "I got to call my sister. Where is my phone?"

He dialed her number.

"Sister! The woman I was telling you about, her name is Lisa, not Lolo! Hilarious!"

There you have it—the birth of Lolo. Rodney and I are still awesome friends, even though we moved on into other relationships. He still calls me Lolo.

The Fantasy Maker

The fantasy man wants to create the perfect life for you. My experience with this dude was short-lived. His mind was Fifty Shades of Crazy.

"Tristan" messaged me, and our conversations started out so sweet. He wanted to know my favorite colors, foods, and places to travel. He wanted to know about all my likes and dislikes.

He said, "I love to make my woman happy, and I want her to have everything that she wants or desires to have in her life."

Red sirens started flashing and ringing in my head.

I said, "Oh, that is very nice of you."

So, I asked him questions about what he wanted in a woman.

He said, "That's not important. My goal on the earth is to make the woman I am with feel important and wanted."

Hmmm, I started to feel a little claustrophobic just through the messages.

"Tristan, please tell me what you are seeking; a relationship is two-sided, so I would like to see if we are even compatible. Our conversation has been all about me. Come on, tell me."

He said, "Well, I want to have a fairytale life with a woman."

"What does that mean?" I asked.

"I want her to be the queen of the castle, and I will be the king. The king will dictate the foundation of the castle, and the queen will delight in making her king as happy as she can."

"Wow, so does this queen work?"

"Oh no, she is a stay-at-home queen, and she will not have servants as she will take care of the castle and all the king's needs."

"So, Tristan, what if I told you I hate to cook? How would that suit you?"

"You will just have to learn to cook and clean to my standards."

I kept pressing him to see to what level the king's anger could be pushed.

"I have a career that I am pursuing, and I will rarely be at home."

"LISA, YOU WILL DO NOTHING THAT WILL GO AGAINST MY WISHES!"

Needless to say, the king was dethroned and thrown into cyber land. The beauty of online dating is the delete and block button.

Goodbye, King Tristan!

A Message from Lolo

Lisa, what do you really want in a relationship? I remember thinking the most important thing to me was a man that had his own relationship with the Lord. I soon learned that this was an inaccurate thought.

I met someone who had such a relationship with God that he made everything about God's likes and dislikes. For example, as he and I were driving to dinner, I noticed a new building was going up. I said, "I love the shape of that building. It's unique."

This guy said, "You are such a disrespectful woman to God. You love a building; don't you know God is a jealous God?"

"What? I'm disrespectful because I like the architecture of a building?"

He was like that about everything. We argued all the time, and I don't even argue. He had "his own relationship with God" for real. None of it made sense to anyone but him. He took every conversation out of context and flipped scriptures around to fit his crazy thought process.

Watch your words and requests.

The Holy Roller

When you enter a message on your profile, and someone sees that you love God and seek the same in a man, some men take it to the crazy level.

Harold messaged me. His first line was, "Hello, beautiful woman of God."

I looked at his profile, and his message was intriguing. He loved the Lord, sports, and church activities. He had four kids, and all were under the age of seventeen; they were his world. That was fine, although my kids were in their twenties. I was curious to see where it would go. So, I responded and thanked him for the compliment.

He replied, "You are an enchanting vision of God."

"Wow! Thank you. I don't think I have ever heard that before, but I'll take it. Harold, I do not see a picture on your profile. Typically, I do not talk to men that don't have a picture since I provided several."

"It's not about that. It's about the heart. God's love sees the heart first and the outer last," he replied.

Despite his lack of photos, my first thought with anyone is to see where it goes.

Harold asked, "Were you married when you had your children?"

I thought that was odd, but okay. I replied, "Yes, and I quickly divorced afterward."

"Divorce is of the devil, and God did not design for man and woman to be divorced."

"Well, Harold, my husband cheated on me. So, I am justified in my divorce by the word."

"Back in the old days, a man could do whatever, and a woman would just deal with the situation to keep her family together," he replied.

I could feel myself getting irritated. I explained to him, "I would not allow my children to see me live in misery and think it was okay."

"Maybe we should talk on the phone because your words seem a little aggressive," he responded.

I also wanted to hear what this dude sounded like on the phone because it's easy for things to get lost in translation with messages. I gave Harold my number, and he called immediately.

"Hello, beautiful!"

"Hello," I replied.

He wanted to jump right back into the conversation about marriage and the dos and don'ts of a relationship.

"Ms. Beautiful, I wanted to go over some scriptures with you about divorce."

While he was preaching and quoting scripture, I went back and looked at his profile to see if he had been married to the mother of those four kids. I was quiet for about twenty minutes, and finally, he took a breath to see if I was still listening.

"Are you there?" he asked.

"Yes. You seem to like to talk a lot, so I'm just listening."

"Do you see the error of your ways of getting a divorce and not working it out?"

"Harold, may I have a minute to ask you a question?"

"Sure, pretty lady."

"When you saw my profile, were you intrigued by it?"

"Yes, I thought, she is beautiful, and I could build something with her."

I said, "If I had not gotten divorced, I would not be on this site, and we would have never met. Are you on this site to meet someone or to preach to women about what you feel about their lives? Did you have those four kids with a wife?"

"No, I was out there in the world and got them."

"Exactly how many baby mommas do you have?"

He said, "Four."

"So, I want to encourage you to be mindful of your past and do not be so quick to pass judgment on others for what you feel they should have done with their lives."

He said, "I am just trying to help you be better and understand the word of God."

"How long have you been ministering?"

Harold replied, "A little over five years."

"How old is your youngest child?" I asked.

"That's neither here nor there," he responded.

"How old?" I questioned again.

He said, "Three."

"What? You want to preach to me about getting a divorce twenty years ago. Yet, you fornicated within the five years you have been preaching and produced a child. Did you think I wasn't paying attention? Harold, thanks for the message and the call, but have a nice life and good luck finding a woman of interest."

Blocked!

The Widower

The widowed man was a special person, and I liked him. Let's call him Christian. His profile was so sweet, and he read to be a humble, kind person. He was Italian, and he was so dang handsome with dark eyes, a thick head of black wavy hair, and deep dimples. That smile! Goodness!

I described him so you can feel what I felt when I looked at him. Christian was the bomb diggity! I saved his profile in my favorites because I wanted to make sure I got back to him to chat later.

I finally got back online later that evening and messaged him. He was online, and he messaged me right back. I was so excited! He told me he wanted to take a moment to read my profile. He would get back to me within the hour. As fine as he is, I thought he's probably talking to many women at the same time. Sure enough, Christian messaged me right back in an hour.

He said, "I would like to let you know that I have been searching for a woman that sounds just like you."

Deep inside, I was very excited and wanted to pursue this "fineness." That may be shallow, but I promise that was all I could see. I calmed down and re-read his profile while he was on a call. Ummm, he was working for Chevron on an oil rig in the middle of an ocean? He also has full custody of a ten-year-old son. How is this possible?

Dang, I have to take those dimpled glasses off and listen. Here we go. Christian returned to the line and began to tell me he loves the fact that I love to travel, and I appear to adapt well to people.

He said, "Lisa, I have a son that I have full custody of, and he is everything to me. His mother passed away in an auto accident, and neither of us has anyone but each other."

My brain started turning with questions, but my spirit said, just listen.

Christian told me he is very active in his son's life, and no cost is too great for him to further his life and future. He paused and asked, "Are you there?"

"Yes, I'm just listening."

His voice was deep and hypnotic in the rhythm of his words.

"Lisa, I want you to promise to give me all of you and love me with all that you have within you. I will reciprocate the same. I must feel love to stay in love. I think that you could be the one I have been waiting for all my life."

I'm thinking, ugh, I haven't spoken twenty words, and he loves me already. Houston, we have a problem.

He said, "So tell me about yourself."

I began with I have two children and one grandchild.

He said, "Family is the seasoning of life's recipe. What do you do for a living?"

"I am a manager in a hotel."

He asked me if I would like to have one of my own.

"Yes, I would like a twenty-bedroom bed and breakfast with all meals cooked on the property and for the dwelling to be the peace that travelers need."

"My deceased wife wanted to have a hotel, and she was sweet like you."

"How old was she when she passed?"

"She was only thirty years old."

"When did she pass?" I asked.

"A year ago," he answered.

"How long were you guys married?"

"Well, we were married for about three years. She was the only woman I have ever been with sexually."

"Whoa, buddy. I didn't ask that question."

He said, "I know, but sex is important to me. I want my son to have a brother or sister."

"Christian, we have been messaging for about one hour. Don't you think it's kind of soon to be talking about sex and extended families?"

"No, my wife and I had sex for the first time on our wedding night, and she got pregnant with my son.

The room started turning red with huge stop signs all over the place. Bells and whistles were ringing in my head. I continued to listen to the "nonmathematician." He was fine but nevertheless a liar.

"Christian, where do you work?"

"I work for an oil company, and I go to different locations to make sure the pipes are functioning properly."

"So, you travel with work?"

I wanted him to say he was stuck in the middle of an ocean somewhere; this statement is a sure sign that a scam is on the way.

He said, "Yes, I am gone for six to nine months of the

year.

"Christian, just so I am clear. You have a ten-year-old son with a woman you were only married to for three years and you were a virgin when you got married. You love your son and are heavily involved in his life. You don't have family on either side, so who is watching your kid while you are traveling for six to nine months a year?"

There was silence, then the connection dropped. Yes, I will let him get the next batch of words together and wait for his call. He didn't appear to be the type just to let me get the best of him without a strong rebuttal. I went on with my day, and he chimed in around four hours later, stating that we need to Skype so that I can see the sincerity in his eyes as we speak.

I thought, don't try to pull that, "She will forget the facts hypnotic crap once she sees me in person." Just because I was so curious to hear his story, I sent him my Skype name. Immediately he rang in, and he was finer in person than in the photo. Hold it together, Lolo. Not everything that looks good is good.

He said, "Now, to answer your questions."

He started with how beautiful my lips are and how my eyes are as black as a genuine piece of onyx.

"First off, my lips have nothing to do with the math in your story. Thanks anyway."

He looked stunned. I giggled inside. Did he think he was going to Jedi mind trick me with a compliment about these lips that I see every day? Not today, your royal fineness.

He said, "Dearest, I didn't want you to leave me, so I didn't want to tell you I was at sea for that long. My son is in military school, so he stays with his friends when he is out at different times of the year. I love him, but I have to work. My wife and I had him years before we got married. I was a virgin when we went out on our first date, and that is when she got pregnant. We did not marry at that time because I was out at sea."

"Why did you feel the need to lie about that?" I asked.

He said, "I didn't want you to think I was a scoundrel of a man."

"I still think that, though, because you asked me about sex immediately."

"You are very combative."

"No, I am just not with the bull crap, Christian."

Then it happened.

"I am not used to women questioning me to this degree after we Skype."

"Oh, really? Well, there is a first time for everything, sir."

He said, "You could have been my one and only true love, and we could have lived a great life. I am a multi-millionaire."

"That's nice," was my response.

There was no reaction from me. Oh, that sent him into a crazy spiral right on Skype.

He said, "Do you not care that you may never have to work again because of my money? All you will have to do is help to see about my son when he is home and while I am working so hard to make a living for our new family.

This guy can't even keep all his lies together.

I leaned back in my chair and looked deep into the camera, and asked, "If you are a multi-millionaire, why are you working so hard in an active job that keeps you away from your son? You should be investing your money and allowing it to work for you. And, possibly working on a business idea that you can open and provide jobs for others yet still brings in another stream of income while you are physically at home with your son and being an active part of his life."

He just sat there and looked at me and said, "I am no longer interested in you or this conversation."

I giggled because some men think their looks will stop you from paying attention to the web of lies, they are spinning.

He Blocked Me.

A Message from Lolo

When you are hiking on a known trail, there will be signs on the trees to let you know which path to follow to fit your physical ability.

In the jungle of online dating, your intuition is your road map. You must pay attention to everything, and if you choose to meet them in person, you can watch their actions. Some can make you lose your way because now all the lights are shining on them. They love what you love, and it is all good. Keep watching. You will surely find out who they are, and then you can decide if their actions and words are a match. A trickster cannot keep his game going for extended periods. Take it easy and wait.

The Trickster

This jungle adventure was quite entertaining. Let's call him "Dennis or DC." He prefers the initials over his full name. This should be fun.

Dennis appeared on my timeline as the Creeper; this was his profile name. Usually, I would delete men with names like this because, in my opinion, if they chose it, there is some truth to it. I read his profile. He had a Master's in Communication, and his photos were very respectful. There were pictures with his mom, kids, and friends. His name went totally against the categories on his profile.

He sent me a message stating that he would love to meet me and maybe take in a play or movie. A play? My interest was piqued.

I returned his message to greet him and to see if he would like to chat later. We chose 4 pm to chat online.

He said, "I don't like all this messaging back and forth, so may I have your phone number?

I liked that approach because it let me know he was a communicator. I forwarded my phone number, and he called right away. He had a soft voice, which was a huge turnoff for me, but okay, let's not be too critical.

He said he liked all my online photos, and he googled me to make sure I wasn't an ax murder.

"How did you do that?" I asked.

"I looked on Amazon for the book you wrote and got your full name and did it that way."

Interesting. He is doing good so far. We talked for almost two hours before he asked, "Are you hungry? It's dinnertime, and I'm hungry."

"I am hungry, actually," I replied.

"Well, if you don't have plans, can I meet you somewhere for dinner?"

"That will work for me."

I chose the area, and he chose the restaurant.

"This is not the side of town you live on, is it?" he asked curiously.

"No, how did you figure that out?"

"You seem secretive, so I figured as much."

I laughed it off without further comment. We ended up at The Public House, which is one of my favorites. I chose downtown, so if any weirdness happened, I could hop right over to The Chattanoogan, a hotel that I worked at for years, where I would feel safe. My co-workers would be all over him like white on rice if he tried anything weird with me.

We had an excellent time and talked about everything under the sun. He told me he used to be an actor when he was in college. That is a passion of mine also, so that opened a deeper conversation. Before we left, he asked if I would like to see Hamilton or The Lion King in Atlanta when it comes in the spring. I was impressed! It was a delightful evening.

"Sure, that would be great!" I answered with a smile.

When we got ready to leave, he said, "If you need anything before you get home, please call me, and I will come to you. I will be on alert until you are safe and sound."

Whoa, this was a pleasant change of pace. Did I mention Dennis was about eight years younger than me? I wasn't expecting this gentlemanlike behavior. Just as I was pulling into the driveway, he called to make sure I was at home.

"I'm walking in."

"Cool, let's talk until you lock the door."

Could it be happening? A possible keeper of the adventure. Let's see what happens.

Over the next few weeks, we enjoyed lots of conversations and dates, movies, dinner, a local play, and a dance recital for his niece.

"I think you need to meet my friends," he said.

At this point, I was so impressed with him, I agreed to the invitation.

"Where are we going?" I asked.

"You'll see. It's a little different from what you are used to. I don't go to places like this often, but this is where everyone is tonight for a school thing.

We went into a club on a back street. You could smell the ribs cooking outside and the marijuana in the smoke mix.

"Are you sure this is the right place?" I asked.

"Come on, woman, let your hair down and live a little."

"Okay, maybe I am acting a little old right now. Let's see how this goes."

We went inside the juke-joint, and everyone

chimed in, "DJ!" You would have thought that President Obama walked into the building. He introduced me as his woman, LJ.

"Y'all catch that, DJ and LJ. That sound good, don't it?" he asked, laughing.

What happened to his correct English that I enjoyed? That fast, Dennis turned into DJ and someone that I did not recognize at all. I was holding on to his hand so tight that he whispered in my ear, "You're safe. I'm not going to let anything happen to you. Trust me, okay?"

I relaxed for a moment until I looked over my shoulder and saw four young ladies looking at me like they were going to shoot me right there on the spot. My instincts and curiosity showed up, and I let go of his hand and went over to the young ladies. I asked if it was okay if I sat with them, and one said no. The others were staring at me.

I asked, "Do one of you ladies date Dennis?

The most evil-eyed one said, "We just broke up, and here he comes in here with an old woman."

Yikes!

I said, "I've only known him for about three weeks."

"Oh, so he was dating you while we were still talking."

Wow, that S.O.B. I apologized to her.

"May I ask you a question?

She calmed down a bit after I apologized.

I continued, "Did he graduate from college?"

"Are you serious?" she asked.

"Yes, ma'am, did he?"

"That fool barely made it out of high school."

I giggled in response. The LIES!!!

"Oh no, did he pull the educated, cultured roll on you?"

"Yes, yes he did," I said. "He is definitely an actor."

She hit my leg.

"Look at him right now."

He was smoking a blunt and drinking straight from a liquor bottle. I looked at her and burst out laughing.

"Lady, you are pretty cool. He is a liar. Wait, did you meet him online?" she asked.

"Yes, I did."

"Girl, you so stupid. That is his brother's profile. Now his brother is more your speed, and he is the graduate."

"But the photos had him in them in the graduation robe," I said, confused.

"Fake," she said as she belly laughed at me. "You didn't give him any money, did you?"

"Heck, no!"

"You better run. His young-minded ass is going to hit you up for all the money that he spent on you. Just look at him. He is probably a different dude than the one you met online and on the phone. That is the real him. He hasn't been over here one time to check on you."

She continued her lesson, "I am going to say something to you, LJ; you don't belong in here, but I am glad that you came so that you can see the truth of this fool. I don't want him, so please don't think that I am doing this to get him back, but I want to save you from this nonsense. Move on and don't look back. At least you found out before he started trying to put pressure on you for truck payments, child support, and rent."

"He would have never gotten it from me," I replied.

We all laughed.

"Do you have Uber on your phone?" she asked.

"Yes."

"Let's get you out of here. One of us would take you, but we have been throwing back shots. He won't even realize you are gone until he gets ready to leave."

We stood up and headed towards the bathroom. The Uber was one minute away, so we slipped outside. She hugged me. I gave her a card and told her to call me if she needed to chat.

"I didn't get your name."

"Chandra," she replied.

"That's a beautiful name, and thank you so much for your help."

"Oh, you not an old lady. I was just mad," she said, smiling.

"I think I am one because this will not work for me," I replied.

She hugged me again, and the Uber driver drove up like a knight on a white horse to take me back to my car.

He still did not know where I lived. Thank goodness! Now that could have gone all kinds of crazy because I knew I did not belong there, but I was curious to see what this was about. An ex-girlfriend of a trickster saved me.

After I got home and changed clothes, I had to take a moment to write the details of this crazy night. Dennis, I mean DJ called me about three hours later.

"Where the hell did you disappear to?

"Oh, now you are cursing at me?"

He was so jacked up on weed and alcohol that he was saying all kinds of stuff.

"Who were you with all that time? I saw you talking to some dudes at the club."

This boy started pulling out all the craziness in his head and making them be my issue.

You know what happened, right?

I blocked him online and blocked his number from my phone.

You Are a Lucky Woman

You would think I would be tired of this adventure by now. Honestly, I would like to meet someone to chat with. Interestingly, I'm beginning to recognize the different types of men in the world.

One Saturday, I was scrolling my page, and this guy popped up.

"Hello, beautiful."

"Hello," I replied.

He said, his name is... let's call him Jake.

"Nice to meet you, Jake. My name is Lisa."

"Your profile pictures are awesome, and I like how you worded your profile."

"Thank you, Jake. Do you mind if I take a minute to look at your profile?"

"Please, it is very nice and filled with exciting things," he responded.

I stopped to look at it, and he was correct. He was into skydiving. I've done that and loved it. He was a jet skier and a Pro Bass fisherman. He enjoyed golfing, tennis, and karate. There were nice photos of him in a business suit. I love that part of a man.

I went back to the chat window and told him his page was truly impressive.

"Oh, I know, right?

The arrogance flag shot up in my head. No judgment, Lisa, give him a chance.

"You have so many hobbies. What do you do for a

living, Jake?"

"I work in the contracting business, and I have about one hundred workers under me."

"That's nice. Do you enjoy it?"

"Actually, I do," he responded. "I work hard, and I play hard."

I told him I liked that he went skydiving, and it was one of the most exhilarating things I have ever done.

He said, "Yes, I am on my tenth dive, and I have achieved the requirements and training so that I can do it alone. Now that is an accomplishment."

"Yes, sir, it is. You should be very proud of yourself."

"Have you eaten dinner?" he asked.

"No, I'm not eating dinner tonight."

"I have one of the largest lobsters you have probably ever seen, and I am going to cook it up tonight with my special grilled corn and roasted vegetables."

"That sounds delicious," I replied.

"Well, you should come on to the house and eat dinner with me."

"Okay, this is the first time that I have ever spoken to you in my life, so why would I come to your home for dinner?"

He said, "Loosen up. It's just dinner."

"Well, I am going to get off of here for the night so you can cook and enjoy your meal."

"So you're really not coming?"

"That is correct. Nice chatting with you."

The following day at 5:40 am, Jake sent me a message asking me to meet him for lunch in Cleveland, TN. Cleveland is about thirty to forty-five minutes away from Chattanooga, TN. When I saw the message, I was at work and messaged him that I work a full-time job, so I would have to bow out of lunch. Then I thought about it. Does he live in Cleveland?

"Jake, do you live in Cleveland?

"Yes, I am very fortunate that I live about fifteen minutes from my job."

Do you see a pattern here, folks? He wants me to come to him and put effort into him early in the adventure. I noticed, but I didn't say anything at the time.

He continued, "I do not come to Chattanooga much, only on Saturday and Sunday for my tennis matches."

"That's nice," I responded.

He was getting very agitated that I was not adhering to his invitations.

"I guess the only way I am going to get to meet you is to come up there."

"You are so right, Jake."

I had him meet me at my job since he wanted to tour my meeting space at my hotel anyway for his company's possible meeting in the spring. He was polite and nice-looking.

After the tour, he asked, "So do you want to ride back to Cleveland with me after my tennis match and stay over until I come back on Sunday."

"I most certainly do not, sir." I couldn't take it anymore. "What kind of women are you used to dealing with, Jake? Women that jump at your beck and call or empty-headed girls?"

"I don't mean to come across like that, Lisa."

Now that caught me off guard, so I settled down but did not forget his arrogance.

A couple of weeks passed, and I asked him if he would like to attend a Christmas party coming up at my job. He said he would love to. I remained at work and changed clothes for the party. This man did not get there for an hour and a half after the party had started. When he got there, he looked nice but complained incessantly about the drive to Chattanooga.

My sweet friend Angie and Shayla had seats at their table and invited us to sit with them. I introduced him, but he was so distant. I noticed them looking at me side-eyed. He ate his food, and we got up and walked around to get photos taken and check out the poker table.

I looked at him, and he was clearly looking at other women. I thought you have got to be kidding me. This is Jake the Jerk. This night was so painful to my soul. When it was over, he asked if I drove to work.

"No, my daughter brought me."

Like clockwork, my phone rang, and she wanted to know if it was time to pick me up.

He said, "I'll take you home.

I told her, and she asked, "What is his name again? Give me his phone number and let him know I am crazy."

I made it home without incident and too much irritation.

"May I come in for a minute?"

"Sure," I replied.

He came in and met my grandkids before they went to bed. He sat on my couch and said the party was boring. I agreed. It was a bit different from the parties that we have had in the past.

"Girl, I had to go through hell and high water to get here for you."

"I will remember in the future." (Not that you will be around for anything else with me, buddy.)

Here is the kicker. I went to the bathroom and spoke to my daughter for a few minutes. I came back, and this boy was snoring on my couch. Really, dude! I gently woke him up and said thanks for attending the party with me. I have to work in the morning, so be safe on your thirty-minute drive home.

Monday morning, bright and early as I was preparing for my day, Shayla came in and asked if I had a minute.

She said, "That dude you brought to the party. Do you like him?"

"Why do you ask?"

I knew why.

"He was horrible! I did not like him for you, and it felt like he thought he was superior to the rest of us at the table. He is so unworthy to even hang out with you or us," she said blurted.

I laughed and told her I couldn't agree more. I told

her about him falling asleep on my couch.

Surprised, she asked, "You let him take you home?

"Yes, as arrogant as he is, it doesn't matter. I won't have to worry about him popping up at my house. He is too proud for that behavior."

She said, "Good, my work is done here."

A month passed, and I got a text from Jake.

"Lisa, it is amazing to me that I have not heard from you."

"Why is that, Sir?"

"Because usually after a date, the women contact me for further engagements."

I just looked at the phone in utter amazement. What a butt head! I said to myself. Let me call this bozo.

He answered, saying, "I knew you would call."

"Really now?"

"Of course, a girl like you. You are lucky that I chose to message you in the first place."

Lord, I am about to find him and beat him up. What was I thinking?

"Why is that, Jake?"

He replied, "Your job is mediocre, your friends are boring, and you need to be more active."

Did he call me fat?

"Wow, well, let me enlighten you, Jake. You are the master of arrogance. You are boring unless you are speaking about yourself. I actually just lost one hundred pounds, and I am very happy with myself, and my friends think you suck.

I adore my job because I get an opportunity to put someone else's needs ahead of mine. That makes them happy, so that makes my soul happy. God has always provided a way for me despite what I see in the natural, so you are fortunate to have been in the presence of a person with a loving, content, and happy soul. You were blessed to be around friends that love through the highs and lows of genuine friendship."

Silence

"Can I buy a vowel right now? It appears you have lost your vast opinions and inaccurate observations about things that are real as opposed to the superficial nature of your life. I bid you farewell, and I hope you find what you are looking for in a woman, but I would advise you to search yourself first for a real personality. Bye-Bye!

Message from Lolo

There are many types of personalities on an online dating adventure. Because of my love and caring nature, this guy is probably one of the worst on my journey. Did he want a woman to date, or did he want a woman to worship him as a great god of the earth? He focused on material things and not matters of the heart, which is the polar opposite of me. I love things, but I love the hearts of people first.

Exchange of Ethnicity or Confused

I was cruising my page and checking out who was online and *ring*. It was a notification from "Brad." Brad's profile picture was of a 1979 Cutlass with big rims. It was clean. I love old cars, and this was my very first car.

He greeted me, "Hello, Sista."

Okay, let's see where this is going. The way he spelled sista made me wonder what he looked like because he didn't have a picture of himself on his profile.

I greeted him.

"Hello, sir. How are you?"

"I'm chillin'. Ain't got nothing going on today," he replied.

First off, chillin' and ain't got? Ugh!

He continued, "Shawty, you are cute as hell."

I rolled my eyes.

"Thank you."

By this time, I was ready to end the conversation and quit responding. But I had to see if he was black or white just out of sheer curiosity.

I said, "Brad, you don't have a picture of yourself in your profile, and I generally don't chat with people if I can't see them. I think it's one-sided since I have several photos on my profile."

He said, "My bad," and sent me a photo directly to my messenger.

He was about thirty years old, a young white guy

with his hat turned backward.

"Brad, I think I may be a little too old for you."

"No, don't do that. I loves the brown ladies. Ain't nothing like having a fine ass Black woman on your arm," he responded.

"I am fifteen years your senior, so I'm probably not the one for you."

He was a persistent young man. So, over the next few days, he would message me several times during the day. I noticed that when we talked about his work, he was very professional and detailed in his speech. I tried to keep the conversation on that level just to understand what in the world he was saying to me.

Side note, when I was growing up, I did not fit into the stereotypical expectations from other races, so some things were challenging for me to understand.

I mentioned to him that I worked in a hotel. He took it upon himself to come for lunch and meet me. I did not have time to have lunch with him, so I took him on a tour so he could report back to his company that we provide meeting space for companies and their teams. I am always working.

"This is dope," he said.

"I haven't heard that term in years! How old are you again?"

"Thirty-one this year. Age ain't nothing but a number, Shawty. Can we sit down for a minute?"

We did.

"What's your favorite food?" he asked.

"I love crab legs and seared scallops?"

"What? Why you eat that stuff?" he asked disgustedly.

"Because I like it."

"What's your favorite dessert?"

"Crème Brule."

"What the heck is that?"

"Oh my goodness! Brad, what is your favorite food?"

"When I'm chillin' at the crib. I like a good ole' tomato and mayo sandwich on white bread."

"I have never eaten that in my life. That is your food of choice?"

"I am a great cook, though. When I feel like it, I will get me some neck bones, sauerkraut, some good ole' mustard greens, and I sit it down."

"Oh, you cook like that? That's nice."

He said, "My chitterlings are the bomb!"

"Brad, are you using these things because this is what you think all Black people eat?"

"No, girl, I just love that food. I make the sweetest Kool-Aid, and man, all that together makes me happy. What is your favorite Kool-Aid?"

I really thought he was just trying to impress me or something.

"Not thinking I am better than anyone, but to be honest, I did not drink Kool-Aid until I got to college or was at a friend's house. My mother never fixed that when I was growing up, and I didn't fix it for my kids.

Brad, if this is who you are, that's cool. But if this is

your conversation for Black women, you should probably think about changing it a little. I am an older woman and totally about business, but I like to have fun conversations as well. I have to understand what is being said to me.

If you approach another woman in my age bracket, never call them Shawty. You and I are the same height. If your game is to be relational per the stereotypical things people think Black people do, you may want to research a little more.

I don't mean to be cruel, but I would like you to use this time as a learning moment if you are seeking any woman at all. And if you want a Black woman, you have got to lose the stereotypes and the lingo. It's insulting."

Brad sat there quietly before responding.

"But I have been in a relationship with plenty of Black women, and they have never said anything. I got their hair and nails done, cooked soul food for them, and they were happy."

"How old were they? Younger than me, right?"

"Yeah, in their twenties."

"For some women at that age, that is refreshing and nice. At that age, this would have been very flattering for me as well. I'm almost forty-five, and I need intellectual conversation. I do not get my hair done, and I hate going to the nail shop. I don't eat any of the food you mentioned, so what are you bringing to my table?"

Brad said it was time for him to get back to work, and he enjoyed our visit.

"You are very uptight, and maybe you don't want a

relationship with a real dude. But I will take note of some of the stuff you said."

"I am working on my uptightness, and I promise I want a relationship with a real dude, but what's real for some is not real for me. We are all out here seeking someone that fits close to our personality and our life. Thanks for stopping by to see me," I responded.

"Dang, just like that, I'm dismissed? Can I at least get a hug?" he asked.

"Oh, sure. I'm a hugger."

"Bye, Brad."

You Remind Me of...

When you are online dating, you never know what people are looking for to fulfill their hearts and souls. This sweet man, "Seth," was an enjoyable experience in my adventure. His story is not long but necessary.

Seth was an older man, and he was humble in all his messages. Seth greeted me one day with, "Hello, Ms. LJ. My name is Seth."

"Hello Seth, how are you?"

"I am doing pretty good today. It's sweltering out here, and I was thinking about getting in the pool a bit."

"That sounds refreshing."

"What are you doing today?" he asked.

"Today, I think I am going to go for a walk and just be in the moment. It's been a very long and busy week."

He said, "Well, if you feel like chatting a little later, here is my number. If I don't hear from you, I'll probably drop you a line on the site. No problem if you are not interested. I know I'm just a little old guy with nothing going on, and you seem to be a very busy lady just from looking at your pictures."

"Do you text?" I asked.

"Yes, I do," he replied.

"Good, I will chat with you a little later."

I made myself go for a walk in ninety-nine-degree weather and truly be in a moment of silence from within. I remember that walk like it was yesterday. Although it was so hot, I was in the stream of a breeze now and then. I thought about Seth's humbleness and how much courage it takes for people to be online and approach a straight stranger with the hopes of something being fulfilled.

When I got home and changed, I sent Seth a text.

He shot back, "Well, L.J., you surprised me. I honestly didn't think that you would contact me back today."

I couldn't put my finger on it, but I wanted to chat with him. After finding out about his kids, grands, and the industry he retired from, he asked if he could call me. I told him that would be fine.

Seth called, and we spoke about everything under the sun. He told me that a nanny raised him, and she was a wonderful woman. When he spoke of her, you could hear the love in his voice for this woman.

He said, "If I am to be completely honest with you, your eyes and smile are identical to hers. She was fair-skinned like yourself. When I was growing up, I kept a small tan because we lived on a lake, and I stayed outside. People would stare at us because they couldn't tell if she was my mom or a caregiver. My mom was so busy with her life that she pretty much turned me over to what she called "the help." I called her my saving grace. My nanny's name was Lilly Sue. She was my mom."

His story was so beautiful. When I looked at the clock, we had been on the phone for two hours.

"LJ, let me quit babbling and let you get some rest. May I text you tomorrow?"

"Sure, Seth, I will look forward to it."

After about a week, he asked, "Would you have lunch with me? You can pick the place."

I got there early and sat in front of the restaurant. Right on time! A short, little man with lovely gray hair walked through the door. He came straight over to me and hugged me. He kind of stayed there for a second and then pulled away with an, "I'm sorry."

I said, "It's okay."

We met at a meat and three-type restaurant. The looks we got from the people were interesting, but I didn't care. The server was rude to me at first, and then I complimented her on her hair to see if she would lighten up a little.

Seth said, "If she had not changed her interaction with you, we were about to have a problem with her, and she was going to have a problem with a tip."

We both laughed and went on to have a great lunch and an excellent conversation. When I looked up one time, Seth was just staring at me with tear-filled eyes. His eyes were as blue as the clearest ocean.

"What's wrong?" I asked.

"Your spirit is just like Lilly Sue's, and you can feel the kindness rolling from you into the room. That is why the server couldn't stay hateful with you because she could feel it, too."

"That is so sweet, and thank you."

"I have to be honest with you. The only reason I messaged you is because you remind me of someone that I loved dearly. She died, and I am having a tough time dealing with it. Even though I am an old man, my heart still breaks. Can you understand that, LJ?"

"Yes, Sir. I can."

This part of the adventure was a sweet memory. Seth allowed me to see that everyone that came online was looking for specific things. I am thankful that I was able to experience this one.

Sexy Photo

I was scrolling my messages on my lunch break, and I got a note from "Rideyouhard69."

"Hey, Sexy Lady."

"Hello, Sir."

"You got some big sexy lips," he commented.

"Ummm, thank you?"

"I bet you can do a lot with those thangs."

I sat looking at the screen in complete silence.

He continued, "I've seen you around here, and me and my boys want to holla at you one night."

I chimed in, "What do you mean exactly?"

"I know you be at all the city stuff, and if you around that many people all the time, you could spend some time with me and my boys."

I was thinking to myself, Stalker! 911! I can't just block him. What if he is a psycho for real?

"Would you like a private picture of me?" I asked.

"Hell yeah!" he replied. Why don't you put on that red lipstick and eat a banana slowly?"

"I got you. I know what you want."

I sent a picture of the Police Chief and me.

He responded, "My bad, ma'am! I will not be contacting you again!"

the
Lenor H

Message from Lolo

Online dating offers a myriad of emotions and self-reflection. I had to ask myself a question. Are you fulfilled in your life with or without a mate?

As I look back to when I first started online dating, I was broken and trying to find myself. When you are empty, you can't expect another person to fill you up. You need to be a complete person before bringing another person into your life.

Broken people draw broken people.

Abandoned

To fall in love with someone and they leave you for no reason is one of the worst feelings, especially when your heart is in "hopeful" love.

I did not date for a long time and I spent thirteen years raising my kids and being their momma. I was working and trying to figure out how to make the income meet the outgoing financial demands. Kids, work, church, and network marketing, that was it.

It was a Ferris wheel ride I stayed on until one day, my son said, "Momma, you need a man. Go out, go online, do something. Sissy and I are good."

I had been online but was scared to respond to anyone. I had lost a total of one hundred pounds. I was in the groove of being a little smaller, wearing different clothes, and feeling good about myself.

I saw a guy online, and his profile piqued my interest, but he had a gang of kids around him. My first thought was, good gosh, what if all these kids are his? I kept scrolling.

That Friday night, one girl I worked with was leaving the company. We went to a restaurant for a farewell dinner and drinks. The topic of online dating came up, and I listened to some of the ladies and men discuss their experience with it.

My friend, Traci, chimed in.

"You people get on my nerves with all of these requirements for a partner. What if you are overlooking a nice man or woman because every one of your requirements is not met?"

I thought, well, is this a word that I should give mister gang of kids a try? That night, I kept thinking about what she said, and I sent him a simple message that said hello.

He immediately responded.

"Hey, pretty lady. How are you?"

"I'm fine," I replied.

"Yes, you are."

That made me blush a little.

I continued.

"I noticed all the kids you have in your profile picture. Are they yours?"

"Girl, no! My kids are grown, and one is in high school. Did that scare you?"

"How did you know?" I asked.

"No one asks that unless they are done with rearing kids. That's cool because as soon as that boy graduates, I am shipping him off to some college. So, breathe, beautiful."

It was late, so I asked if we could chat tomorrow.

He said, "My hands are enormous, and all this messaging is driving me crazy. May I send you my phone number and when you are comfortable you can call me? Or you can text me, and I will make the first phone call."

I liked that thought. He sent his number, and I texted, "good night."

The next day I woke up to his text that read, "Good

morning. I hope you have a day as beautiful as you are. I am looking forward to hearing your voice."

Let's call him Wes.

He texted me around noon and asked if he could call me? I told him, sure. He called, and we chatted like we had known each other forever. It was nice.

"What are you doing this weekend?" he asked.

"I am doing a network marketing meeting with my friend Moses. It's my meeting, so I hope that everyone I invited shows up."

"Can I come down and support you? If you'd like, I'll stay the night and take you on a date if that's okay."

"That sounds awesome," I replied. I snapped into reality and blurted out, "Don't think you are going to bamboozle me in the bed just because you made a trip."

Wes started laughing so hard.

He said, "You haven't dated in a while, and you are paranoid. That is not my intention, and I don't want you to date me from a place of the past or pain. Relax a little, and let's just look forward to getting to know each other. Now, if you can help me find a decent rate for a hotel. I can give you my credit card number."

I called my friend Robin at the Stay Bridge, and she took the reservation.

Wes said, "If anything comes up, you take the room and have a night of sleep on me."

"Are you serious?"

He laughed, "Oh boy, I am going to have fun with you."

My heart was leaping out of my chest, and my brain slowly became involved in this newfound situation.

On Friday, Wes called me.

"I'm here, and I've already checked into my room. If you would like to go to dinner after you get off work, I am at the hotel. Let me know what you want to do, and we will make it happen."

I was so excited to see him face to face. I can't remember what happened at work that day, but I do remember that my director let us leave an hour early. I went home, took a shower, and got dressed for my first date in thirteen years. I did not have a moment of fear, which was odd because my trust level was nonexistent. I texted Wes and told him that I was on my way to the hotel.

He asked, "Do you mind coming upstairs for a minute so we can chat?"

Without hesitation, I said, "Okay."

When I got there, he greeted me with the biggest bear hug. I melted into it like a child greeting her father after he gets home from work.

"Stand back, let me see ya," he said. You are as beautiful as your photos."

I grabbed his hand and looked at it, remembering that he said he couldn't text because his hands were enormous. Yes, I remembered that from our first chat. His hands looked like bear paws. I loved that.

He offered me a seat, and we began talking. An hour passed by so fast. His phone rang, and I heard him say, "Hey, my friend. I am in Chattanooga. I was about to take my girl to dinner, but we can swing by."

When he hung up the phone, he said I hope you don't mind. My good friend Corey lives here, and I really want to see him today, so I can focus on you tomorrow and leave afterward.

Lolo Note: This feeling was overwhelming, and I enjoyed every moment. A man who seemed to be a leader. I was so tired of being the leader of every single decision in my life. So, I just vanished into this emotion.

He put me in the car. We put the address in Google maps, and off we went. We listened to Maze and enjoyed great conversation, laughing all the way to Corey's house.

When his friend opened the door, they belly laughed and hugged each other like long-lost brothers.

Corey's wife said, "Y'all get out the way and let the lady in the house."

Wes said, "I'm sorry, baby."

Corey's wife asked if we wanted something to drink and disappeared into the kitchen. Wes and Corey were chatting it up, and I was texting my kids to tell them where I was, just in case. Then I heard Wes say, "Man, are you looking at my girl's legs?"

Corey replied, "As a matter of fact, I am. They are pretty."

"Dang, man, I just got her. Where is your wife?"

We all laughed, and his wife came back into the room with wine, cheese, and crackers. We talked for about an hour.

Wes said, "We need to go. I need to feed my baby

and get her home."

We went to Red Lobster, and he started ordering so much stuff.

I said, "Wait, I can only eat something small. I had gastric bypass surgery and can barely eat anything since we ate at Corey's."

"Oh no! I love to cook and eat, and my woman eats like a toddler."

We both laughed.

We had a fantastic night out. It was like we had known each other forever.

When we got back to the hotel, he said, "It's getting late, but I am not ready for you to leave. Is that selfish?"

"No, because I am not ready to go."

Yikes, Lolo. You are rolling on straight emotion. I didn't care. I was going up. We walked to the room, and I sat on the couch. He bought wine and fruit. I took my heels off and sat cross-legged on the couch with my dress firmly tucked under my knees. He brought over the wine and fruit, and we talked about our kids and life goals.

Oh my goodness! I got a cramp in my leg. I jumped up, and it must have scared him.

"What's wrong?"

I couldn't even speak. I pointed to my leg. He jumped up and got a hot towel, and sat me down. He began to massage my leg with the towel. Those paws had magical powers!

"Let me massage your feet."

Well, he already had one on his lap, so why not? It

felt delightful. I must have been tired as heck because I woke up in bed under the covers, fully clothed. He was on the couch with the paper over his chest. It was 4 am, and my meeting was at 9. I woke him up and thanked him for an awesome night.

"It's too late for you to drive home alone."

"I have to leave. I need to get some notes together for my meeting, and you should get some rest also."

He said, "If you have to, I am going to follow you home, okay."

When we got to my apartment, he got out, opened the door, and stood right there until I got into the house. I was torn between being impressed and wondering if I was having a game run on me. His heart felt so genuine. I decided to just roll with it.

He texted to let me know he had made it back to the hotel and asked if I would like to come over in the morning to have breakfast and go over my notes.

That would be lovely.

I got back to the hotel around 7:30. He was up and dressed. He met me downstairs.

He said, "You look beautiful and super professional."

Wes was about 6'3 and 280 pounds. He had a bald head, a gray beard, and beautiful skin. When he bent down to hug me, it was a welcomed event. Did I mention that he smelled terrific?

"I know you will not eat much. I'll get your food and coffee, and you pull out your notes," he said.

I could get used to this treatment. I had known him

for less than a week, and it felt like a lifetime. We ate, and I had a perfect cup of coffee that I did not have to fix. He listened to my opening welcome and the introduction of the guest speaker. I explained the business to him, and he was really interested.

We got to the meeting early and greeted the speaker. Wes put the programs in the seats and set up the registration book for the visitors. We were a tag team, and it felt so good to have someone understand the process of my mind and what I was hoping to accomplish with this company.

While I was speaking, Wes looked at me with those beautiful eyes as if he were so proud of me. Those big paws clapped so loud for me as I took my seat. Although only ten people showed up, the meeting was a success. It was still a great beginning for me.

We left the meeting and went back to his hotel. I asked if he needed help getting his things together. He said he packed earlier and put everything in the truck. He just wanted to spend a little more time with me without distraction.

"I asked for a late checkout," he said.

I thought to myself; I know he doesn't think he is fixing to get any of my girlie.

I must have tensed completely up because he said, "Don't worry, honey. I will not attack you. I would like to kiss you, though. If that is okay."

I felt it was okay because I wanted to kiss him as

well. I looked at the clock and remembered saying to myself; it is 11:40, and a late checkout would be 1 pm. Watch yourself, Lisa J.

Wes kissed my forehead, my cheek and slowly kissed my lips. Oh, my goodness! I felt all kinds of things come through my body, mind, and soul. Then he took those big ole paws and held me so tight. I thought I would melt into a puddle on the floor. I backed away from him. I thought, oh, this will not be good for me. I must have given him a seductive, come get me look because he said, "No, ma'am. I promised you I just wanted to kiss you, so you ain't getting none of my junk."

I'm not going to lie; a little tigress came out of me. I push him on the couch, sat on his lap, and continued that kiss until check-out time. Yikes!

I jumped up and said, "Okay, it's time to go, brother."

"Yes, sister, we need to relinquish this room before I have to stay another night."

As we walked to my car, he said, "I hope to see you again very soon."

I said, "Well, I will be in your hometown next week."

"Really? Why?" he asked.

"I am graduating from college next week, and my sweet classmate and her husband have set up a wonderful weekend with me since I will be alone. Graduation is two weeks before Christmas, and my family is going to Myrtle Beach. I did not want them to try to figure out my graduation trip on top of that, so Lindsi included me so I could graduate knowing that I was not alone. You live in Nashville, and I am driving there to spend the night before we travel to graduation about an hour away."

"What hotel?" he asked.

I told him.

He said, "I can be there. It's just thirty minutes from where I live."

So, another date was set, and off we went. We talked every day that week. I texted him to let him know when I got there and checked in.

"I was trying to work it out so that I could drive you to the graduation myself and attend with you. You could have someone else there that thinks the world of you."

He said, "I do have one request if you don't mind. I will be in that part of town at one of my brother's houses until about 8:30 pm. You said you all are going to dinner, so do you mind if I come to your room and wait so that I don't have to drive all the way back home? My brother and his family are going on a trip. They're leaving at night so the kids can sleep on the road."

I did not hesitate to say yes.

Lindsi, her husband, and I went to B.B. Kings Dinner Club. They had an incredible band, and the food was terrific. We had a wonderful time, and I was thankful for the experience.

I left Wes a key at the front desk. When we returned, he was waiting for me in my room watching T.V. He looked so nice. Next came those big arms and the safety of being locked in those big paws. What in the world is this feeling?

I felt like I was sinking into a place of peace of heart but body disruption. I am coming from thirteen years of no-touch, no love, no feelings. After my divorce and joining the Early Church, I was celibate for all that time, so- I pulled away and went to the bathroom to give myself a pep talk. Well, I did not need any pep. I needed to be talked down.

I came back into the room.

Wes said, "Don't worry, baby girl, I got you."

He clearly had to give himself a pep-down talk as well. We laughed at each other.

He said, "I will sit here in this chair, and you sit on the bed. Let's talk."

Thank goodness.

We made it through this visit with music, laughter, and conversation. Wes apologized for not being able to be with me for my graduation. I was just happy to be with him at that moment, as his presence added great joy to the entire trip.

It was getting extremely late.

He said, "Let me get out of here before my gentlemen-like behavior turns cold."

Me and my hot self said, "Can I have a happy graduation kiss before you go?"

"No," he replied.

I disagreed, so I made it happen.

When that kiss ended, an entire hour had passed. How did I end up on this bed with his big arms around me so gently?

"Girl..."

"Boy, goodnight!"

We laughed, and he left.

The first thing that morning, he sent me a happy graduation text. This man was making me happy already. After graduation, I got back into my car at the hotel. I met him at a gas station near my exit to head home. He came to the car and looked at my gas hand.

"Pull over to pump three."

I did, and he filled up my tank. We went into the store.

"Get you something for the road, so you don't have to spend money on snacks or anything before you get home. I don't know what bird eaters eat."

"Oh, you got jokes," I said.

My surgery was only three years old, so I was still sensitive to different foods. I had a lot of can't haves in my diet. I appreciated his regard for that fact.

"You are messing with me, Lisa J. I am so glad that we met."

He put me in the car, kissed my hand and my forehead, and sent me on my way. On my way home, I caught a glimpse of myself in the rearview mirror, and I was smiling for no reason.

The following week was a little different between Wes and me. He only sent a text a couple of times, and I only spoke with him the day I got back home from the graduation trip. I was devastated. I didn't understand how something so sweet that felt so good could fall apart so quickly?

Note from Lolo: If you need a particular type of communication, you need to let it be known to the person you are building with immediately. Their idea of communication may not be what you need to maintain your faith in the relationship.

The following week wasn't any better. I was confused. I called my mom to check on my daddy, and she said he was in hog heaven. I asked what he was doing.

She said, "Wes is clearing the yard of some brush that he wanted to be cleaned up and mowing the grass."

"Who?" I asked, confused.

"Your boyfriend. Didn't you know he was here?"

"No, ma'am, I didn't."

Oh, I forgot to mention that I had to swing by my mom's house to take my dad some medicine on Wes's first night in town. Evidentially, he got their phone number from my dad when mom and I were in the kitchen getting the meds prepared.

"Mom, don't tell him you talked to me and don't even bring me up, okay."

"Why? He's been talking about you all morning. He really likes you," she said.

While I was speaking to her, my cell phone notified me of a text from Wes.

It said, "Hey, baby girl. Sorry about the disconnect. Come by your parents after you get off, okay."

I typed back, "Sure."

He replied, "Don't be mad at me."

When I got off a few hours later, I went to my parents. He was still working in the yard, and it was beautiful. My dad was sitting on the porch, watching and giving directions.

Momma gave Wes a towel and washrag, and he disappeared into the bathroom. He came back out in clean clothes and smelling delightfully yummy. I guess you can tell I love a good-smelling man. I was sitting on the couch when he came out and gently grabbed my hand and said, "Excuse us."

We went on the porch.

"You are such a wonderful woman, and I am an emotional man with no direction. I may not communicate with you all the time, but don't get mad. It's just me."

This would have been a perfect time to say that's not going to work for me, but I didn't say a word. Why? Because I was wrapped up in emotion.

"Sweet Lady, I have to leave now. This was just a trip for Dad and Mom."

He kissed me and went inside to tell my parents goodbye.

We went for a couple of weeks with limited conversation but more texting. It was okay. I was working so much, and I immersed myself in those thoughts.

My company sponsored the Heart Ball, and all of the managers were asked to attend. This was great for me because I wanted to wear my first after-five attire since my surgery. I had a gown that I wore to my best friend Genna's wedding. When she bought it, I had to get a size 28/30. I felt like a fat pig, but I loved that dress. It was long, black with sequins all over it, no sleeves, a high neck, and a split up the thigh. It was beautiful.

I took the dress to my mom's tailor, and she asked me to try it on. It looked like a garbage bag on me. She tightened it up and put giant clothespins in the bag.

She said, "We are going to have to cut a lot of this dress off."

As I stood on the stool in the mirror after she put the pins in the back, I began to silently weep at the new me. I was so proud of myself.

She said, "Girl, quit crying! Be happy."

She was a very bossy but wonderful little Asian lady. She advised me that the dress would be ready on Thursday. That was perfect. The ball was on Saturday night.

I got my hair done in a new style, and I was feeling happy with myself. I thought I would get myself a room for that night and enjoy an evening of quiet time and taking in my new life.

Wes started to feel like a beautiful dream. I thought to myself, let me start getting over it. That was the mindset of a damaged woman.

Thursday came, and Wes called to ask me how I was doing. He apologized for his lack of communication.

I said, "It's cool. But I need to go. Talk to you soon."

"Don't do that, baby girl," he replied.

"No, I really need to get back to work."

I hung up.

He called me on Friday.

"What are you doing this weekend?" he asked.

"I am going to a ball for work. I got me a room so I can get some rest and refocus."

"Okay, that sounds nice. May I call you a little later?"

"Sure," I said casually.

I went to work. Towards the end of the day, my friend Untrice called and said, "Let's have dinner tonight."

On my way to pick up Untrice, Wes called.

"Where are you, baby?"

"I am going to have dinner with a friend," I responded.

"Where are you going? I will go to the same place here in Nashville, and we can eat together."

"That's weird but okay."

I told Untrice what Wes said.

"Okay, talk to your boo while we're on a dinner date."

We went to Ryan's with my granddaughter, Lingy. My daughter worked there, so it was nice to be with them before I was out for the night on Saturday. Not to mention, dinner with Untrice is always a treat. She's so much fun!

The wind was blowing like crazy, and my new hair was being uncooperative. We got into the restaurant and got a seat in Jazmyn's section. After we sat down and got settled, I looked up at Untrice, and she had a strange look on her face. At that moment, I felt a hand on my back. I turned around, and it was Wes! I was so happy to see him. I got up to hug him. That embrace sent all of my anger out of the window.

"What are you doing here?" I asked.

"I got here early this morning. I would like to spend time with you tomorrow after the ball."

"I am angry with you," I said, frustrated.

He whispered in my ear, "Let me make it up to you tomorrow. I'm so sorry."

I introduced him to Untrice, Jazmyn, and Lingy.

"Enjoy your dinner, and I will call you tomorrow morning," he said before leaving.

He hugged me again and was on his way.

The next day was the ball. I checked into my hotel.

Wes called and said, "I'm staying at Corey's because I don't want you to feel obligated to let me stay with you tonight."

"I want you to come and stay with me, but I'm not giving you jack. You feel me?"

I was getting dressed when he knocked on the door. My heart melted in his arms.

I went into the bathroom to finish getting dressed. I could not reach my zipper, so I came out and asked for assistance. After assisting me, he turned me around.

"Damn, you're beautiful."

He then kissed me deeply. It was so passionate and genuine.

"I will drive you over to the event, okay. I will be right here when you get back.

The ball was great, and I thoroughly enjoyed myself.

The food was extraordinary, and the wine pairing was perfect. I was a little light-headed by the time I got back to the hotel. I knocked on the door and almost fell in the room, tripping over my gown.

"Whoa, are you okay?" he asked.

"I'm fine," I said while laughing.

Clearly, I was a little tipsy. I asked him to unzip my dress. I grabbed my robe and sleepwear and went to change.

Hold it together, Lisa. You are playing with fire right now.

Wes met me at the door with a glass of wine and gave me a bouquet of flowers.

"How sweet! Thank you," I said, smiling.

We sat on the couch. I sipped my wine and ate some of the cheese and crackers he had prepared. I had overdone it. I got up and laid in the bed.

"Lisa, may I join you, please?"

I agreed but told him if I ever slept with him, it would not be tonight because I was very tipsy, and I did not want that. His lips covered my lips, and a passionate kiss began. It was freaking awesome.

I turned away and asked him to hold me. I needed to pull it together. He whispered in my ear.

"Lisa, did you know I was at the restaurant last night when you got there?"

"No, you weren't."

"Yes, I was. I watched the way the wind blew your hair as you were getting out of the car and how you stopped and kneeled to button the baby's hood on her head while fighting the wind blowing your hair in your face. Your friend said something to you, and you threw your head back and laughed so loud and so deep. I adore everything about you."

After that weekend, we talked and texted. There were more surprise visits after days of not communicating. I loved him despite the obvious things that I should have been running from appeared.

The year 2012 was awesome and full of emotion for me. I'm going to fast forward to 2013. We planned a trip to Savannah for the first week of November. I took off work, and we saved money. We didn't book a hotel or anything. We were just going to go. We were scheduled to leave on November 8th. He called early that morning, around six, to say he would run a little late and that he would be here around ten.

"No problem, honey, see you then," I said.

The time kept going on, and no Wes. There were no calls or texts from him, and he wasn't responding to mine. Around one that afternoon, he called to say he was not coming.

"Why!" I asked.

He simply said something came up.

"Fine!"

I hung up, kissed my family, got in my car, and went on a solo journey towards Savannah. I cried, but in the same breath, I was proud of myself for leaving anyway. He kept calling me, but I did not want to talk to him until my voice was not shaking with anger and hurt.

I stopped at a gas station somewhere in Georgia, looked over to the left, and saw a brand-new Comfort Inn and Suites. I drove over and asked how much the rooms were. The clerk told me $150.00. I wondered if they had any rates for hoteliers. After finding out about my property and talking and laughing about the ins and outs of the industry, she gave me the room for $80. It was beautiful.

I went back out and got some food and snacks. I returned to the room, took a shower, and got into bed. Wes called.

"I'm sorry, baby girl. What are you doing?"

"Trying to find something on T.V.," I replied.

"Why is it so quiet? Where are the kids?"

"I'm in Georgia at a hotel."

"You went anyway?" he asked, surprised.

"Yes, I was not going to be stuck at home on my first requested week off work in nine years."

He kept apologizing.

"I am tired in my body and soul, Wes. I have to go to sleep."

"No matter what happens, you are so special to me, and you own a big piece of my heart, Lisa."

My soul was so disappointed that I slept for fourteen hours—something that only happens when I'm sick.

Wes texted me on my last day out to make sure I got home. I didn't talk to him again. Abandoned without explanation is a heart-wrenching, confusing place to be when you love someone so much. I moved on in silent pain. I talked to my pastor about it, and he tried to help me. Finally, I prayed that out of all the heartbreaks, I needed this guy to come back and apologize to me.

On May 7, 2017, while working in New Jersey, I searched his name, and a page came up. I had never done that before.

I typed, "Glad to see you are doing well."

He immediately responded.

"I have been looking for you!"

We picked up the conversation as if nothing ever happened, at least until he wanted to come and visit me.

"No, you hurt me, and I will not put myself at risk again with you."

We video chatted often, and on the 26th of May, he sent me this message.

I made the mistake of leaving our relationship because of my paranoia, which I'll have to live with. I can't change the past, and I understand your fear of me. I respect you wanted a committed relationship, and I failed you. I know I was capable of being in a committed relationship with someone, and even though I left you, you were my one. I never thought we were going to end our relationship the way we did. It was not planned. I guess I needed to say that I still have strong feelings for you. I'm sure coming back into your life after what happened would be an emotional roller coaster for you. I just want you to know that all the feelings I had for you were genuine, and they still are. I just want you to be my girl again.

Note from Lolo: God answers our prayers, and I got

my apology. It took four years, but I got it. I had the opportunity to release him from my soul of continuous, unexplained longing.

Wes and I continued to have wonderful conversations and lots of facetime on messenger. On March 27th, we had a quick text. He said, "I hope you are having a good one." I told him I was and that I was clearing my mind and would talk to him later.

He replied, "Go ahead and clear your mind, and let's talk later. I'm going back into the water."

That was the last time we spoke. It didn't dawn on me until my birthday that he didn't tell me Happy Mother's Day or Happy Birthday. I thought, let me call and mess with him. I noticed there was no activity on his messenger, which was odd. I looked at his page and found R.I.P. Just like that, he was gone, for real.

Message from Lolo

If you are really into a relationship with a person from out of town and care for them deeply, make sure there is some contact with a family member or something, just in case an illness occurs. In this story, I knew three people from his family, and two had died. My number changed after we lost contact.

Sugar Momma- Negative

Just because I am older, don't think you are going to get some money from me. One night around three am, I got a message from "Zack."

"What's up, little momma?"

I couldn't sleep that night, so I entertained his message.

I replied, "What's up, youngster?"

"Youngster? I am all the man you will ever need."

I stopped and looked at his profile. Yes, just what I expected. Super young in mind, body, and soul.

I said, "What made you stop by my page. You see my age, and I am old enough to be your momma, right?"

"I need a woman like you. You doing thangs and making money moves," he replied

"Wait, are you looking for a Sugar Momma?"

"Well, I'm going to be laying some serious pipe, so yes, I am."

"Let me school you quick, youngster. I only eat, play, and lay with someone that brings his best to the table. If all you are bringing is the pipe, son, I can purchase that if that was my choice." (I don't choose to, by the way.)

"Bye, User!"

Blocked!

The Resource

Online dating may not bring a love connection but a new idea of collaboration. I met one man online during a challenging time in my life. I had no job and no possibilities, so I thought. Let's call him "Benzo." I saw him online. He was a bit older but seemed nice. We chatted via messenger for a few minutes before he said, "If you don't mind, I would rather talk on the phone."

I replied, "Sure."

He called on October 30th, and we talked for three hours. He had the sexiest voice and excellent intellectual conversation.

He said, "I would like to come and see you tomorrow if you don't mind."

We met at 9:30 that evening at an IHOP and stayed until a little before 2 am.

"I am too tired to drive back to Atlanta tonight," he said sleepily.

I gave him the nearest location for multiple hotels and reserved one. He knew that I was not working, so he informed me of a different job from what I was used to, but sales are sales.

He said, "It's in the real estate business leasing apartments."

"I'm not scared to try, that's for sure."

"I didn't think so. It's a cool position as long as you don't mind traveling and being away from your family for a minimum of thirty days at a time."

"Well, my kids are grown, and there is face time."

"Cool, I will let you know the number next week, okay?"

Afterward, I took him directly to the hotel. He invited me up to finish our conversation. He seemed like a gentleman, so I joined him. We talked like old friends until 4:30.

I said, "This has been refreshing, but I must go."

Because of Benzo, I worked in a new industry, lived in five major cities, stayed in fantastic apartments, and drove nice vehicles. The best part is, I did not pay a dime.

Benzo came to me with this opportunity right after being threatened with eviction from my home. I was headed to live in a hotel for thirty days because I was homeless. The day after I was evicted, I got the call from this company to come to a paid training. I left for my new assignment on January 2, 2017.

Benzo and I tried to push this into a relationship, but I understood not everyone you meet would be a real love connection. He was a resource that helped me move forward with information and a new work adventure in a brand new industry.

Benzo and I are still friends, and he is an awesome man. I wish the absolute best for him and his new love.

Beware

Please beware of this guy. After giving this book to the editor, this story happened, but I have to share it with you.

Have you ever met someone that clicked with your very soul? Well, I totally did! He did not find me on a dating site but a business site. Let's call him "Adam."

Adam was a breath of fresh air. When we spoke, everything just felt right with the world. Adam was an excellent communicator and very complimentary. Some men don't like to face time, but he did, and I found that interesting. Adam and I texted daily and sent pictures. It felt like this relationship might gain some wings soon.

I think what I loved most was that we shared a love for music, and he would send me jokes via text to make me laugh. If he did not have time to talk at that moment, he would send me a quick video just to say hi. He just felt good, and his smile was everything.

My best friend Genna said, "You really like him, don't you? Did you Google him?"

"I did, but I did not find anything."

My history has been, if I like them too much, there may be a huge hidden problem. The deeper I began to feel for him, the more I heard my friend's voice in my head screaming at me.

On Wednesday, I was having a terrible day, so I texted him and asked him to call me. When he called, another personal whirlwind was stirring.

I remember asking, "Oh, are you on your way to church?"

"I am," he replied.

"Can you call me when it's over?"

He paused for a second, then said, "Yes."

I needed something to do to take my mind off what was going on around me. So, I thought I would use this time to investigate him a little more just to feel safe knowing that I was on a good road with him. I went to the page where we met and googled every word I saw that was not pertaining to his job. I noticed in his profile that his full name was not present; it was another name. I cut and paste that name into the search box. Guess what I found?

A church Facebook page came up, and what did I see? He is a pastor of a church, and he had a wife! I was so hurt. I told him upfront I had a small level of trust left in me. I sat there, holding my phone like a zombie. Then my phone rang. It was him.

Of course, my need for him to call had shifted to a new topic.

He said, "Hey, Baby."

I said, "I have a question for you. Are you married?"

There was a pause.

He responded, "No, why would you ask me that?"

I didn't let on that I dug deeper.

I said, "Your church page just popped up on my Facebook page."

There was silence, and the phone went dead.

I began to psycho text him, asking why he would do

this. Why! I told him how I saw a video of him preaching and how his beautiful wife looked like an awesome woman of God. My heart was breaking for her and me.

I was overtaken with the question why! I texted him and asked if he thought I would be an easy target or if he thought I was weak?

Finally, three days later, he texted me and said he didn't think I was an easy woman but a great woman. Deep inside, I was glad that he had the courage to text me. I am very transparent here. I chatted with him for a couple more days. Then it dawned on me that I cared about her and her heart. As a woman, I will not take part in the sorrow of another person on purpose.

To know that he was a pastor and a husband, yet he never acknowledged his wife bothered me. At one point, I even asked him if I was the only one, and he said yes. Did I want to believe it? Yes, I did. However, because of his disrespect for her, I knew that if I took him up on his offers, he would do the same to me, even if he divorced his wife and left his church. I would never trust a word that came out of his mouth.

I was entangled in a web of lies and silent deceit. But still, why? I don't want to accept that he is just a man, and that's how they are.

I'm a hopeless romantic, but this episode has made me step back and be okay with where I am right now. God will provide me with someone in due time, the very one that he designed just for me.

Some women say they are good alone. I can relate to

that, but I also know that in the quiet part of my soul, a God-designed marriage is a desire of my heart.

In the words of Forrest Gump, "That's all I have to say about that." BLOCKED!

Success Story

I had not been on a date in over four years. February 14, 2010, came around, and I took my teenage daughter Anna and my niece Megan out for dinner.

We ate some bad Mexican food for our Valentine's "date." After my second margarita, I announce I was considering online dating. They both let out a shriek and decided we should sign up that night.

Fast forward two hours later. They had given me a make-over, taken my picture, and helped me fill out the forms for Match.com. At forty-one, I decided to be honest, brutally honest. I mean tequila, honest. I was a single mom and a liberal who moved from Vermont to be near family in the Georgia conservative Bible belt. What did I have to lose?

I opened Match.com and causally started checking boxes to create my profile.

- ✓ Single Mom
- ✓ Ultra-liberal
- ✓ Owns two dogs and three cats
- ✓ Moderate Drinker
- ✓ Does not go to church regularly
- ✓ Very curvy (aka code in online dating meaning "overweight")

You get the idea. I did not hold back.

I wrote the paragraph about how I am a bit of a nomad who moved every few years, and my daughter has been my constant travel companion. I was so new to this online thing that my online name was my actual name. I did not know you were supposed to come up with a cute little name for personal protection like "ocean lover." We finished the profile, but we still needed a title for my Match.com profile. We created "Let's see if this works."

I went to hit the charge my credit card button, and I froze. Obviously, the tequila had worn off at this point. I chickened out and said, "Let's post the free profile without the picture, and I will think about it overnight." I had to work early the next day, and when my sister came home from her romantic Valentine's getaway, the girls told her what we were up to. She grabbed her credit card, uploaded my pictures, and she paid for a one-month subscription for me. I was at work, and bam! I had fifty emails from Match.com saying, "so and so is interested." My sister told me what she did, and I laughed and decided to give it a try.

Unbeknownst to me, all the new account members are a kind of "fresh meat" in the online dating world, and by the time I got home, I had 200 "winks." I was totally overwhelmed. I consulted with all the women in the family, and I handed my account over to Anna and Megan. I set rules. No pretending you are me and no messaging or emailing any of the men. They could say yes or no if interested and narrow down the list for me–but that was it.

After school every day, the girls would come home

and comb through the available men between the ages of forty to fifty-five. It was their own version of a reality show. I soon discovered my niece chose the romantic world of firefighters in Wyoming or the handsome Italian men who would "relocate for love." Having lived through all my bad dates and some good and not-so-good boyfriend choices, my daughter had a more pragmatic approach.

After two weeks, I was no longer the new blood on Match, and the emails were down to a trickle, with most of them wanting to "save me" and take me to church. I decided not to renew when the month was up and take a break from the overwhelming world of online dating.

I came home from work, and my daughter, Anna, informed me she had found the guy for me. She said he was perfect! He loves to travel, liberal, loves food and drink, the ocean, and he seems funny.

I took one look and said, "Nope! He is cute but too skinny."

I contacted him anyway, and Greg and I emailed each other for a month, getting to know each other. Greg was charming, smart, flirtatious, and funny. We emailed about books, songs, favorite foods, our past, kids, and dreams. I felt we really got to know each other over that month. I would smile when I would wake up in the morning and see an email from him. We decided to meet up, and he called to set a date.

That first call was awkward. I just shrugged it off, and we met for margaritas and watched the sweet sixteen basketball tournaments after work. We wanted to see if we had the same spark in person that we had in our emails.

I was nervous the afternoon of our first date and during lunch ran to a store to buy a new top to wear. We met up at a local restaurant, and it was, well, awkward. He was in stiff jeans and a button-down. I was nervous in my new sweater, which did not fit very well. We went from the easy banter of the emails to a forced conversation about the weather and the basketball game. We cut it short and said we would talk again in the future.

I was sure this potential romance was done, but we met one more time after work just for fun. He suggested a golf range. Neither of us were golfers, but he had an ancient set of clubs. We met at a casual driving range—no new clothes for me this time. I wore my old yard working capris pants and a t-shirt. He wore his tattered shorts and a t-shirt. We were both much more comfortable in our own skin. Greg packed a picnic with cold wine, beer, and lousy grocery store sushi, which we never opened. We had a blast just hitting buckets of balls and laughing until our sides hurt. I had to leave early and go home to meet the new dog sitter. I invited him to come along and meet the family. I held my breath, and he said yes, he would love to.

We have been together ever since, maybe not the typical relationship, but we have grown with it as well. We had some bumps in the road, with plenty of fights and even more making up.

During those first few years of dating, I got my first passport and visited Italy and France with him when he was working overseas. I met all his family members and his two children in Virginia. His ex-wife and all the family welcomed me with open arms, and we have been friends ever since. In 2012, after dating for two years, Greg, Anna, and I moved in together to create our new family.

In 2013 I traveled to Dubai to meet him during a break from his job, and we got engaged! We took our time and stayed engaged for five years, but as the saying goes, "When you make plans, God laughs." The following month Greg was contracted for several months of guaranteed overseas work and asked me to quit my job and join him. One little catch. We needed to get married fast so I could get a passport to get the necessary business visas to join him. I took a half-day off work. We got married in an impromptu ceremony at the Ringgold wedding chapel on a Tuesday afternoon.

Anna was hiking the AT trail with her cousins when all of this happened. Every time she would get to a cell signal, I would send her updates. Every mountain peak comprised a new life-changing text: quitting my job, getting married tomorrow, and selling the house when you go to college in a couple of months. To this day, she never forgives me for not being at our wedding.

We spent the summer before she started college traveling with Greg's daughters and vacationing with Anna and both families. The day we dropped Anna off at college, we boarded a plane for Qatar and have been living the nomad life ever since.

Has it always been smooth sailing? No! It may look romantic on Facebook and Instagram, but the reality of spending 300 days in a hotel room that first year was a challenge. As work slowed down, we enjoyed our time together, "half-retired."

We had a company of two, and it could be challenging working and living with your spouse 24/7. Our work usually takes us overseas for six months. We explore the US in our small travel trailer, visiting family and friends the other six months. It is an ideal life for us, but not for everyone. We have been lucky enough to visit twenty-five countries and camp in thirty-two states over the last eight years. We hope for many more years to come.

The adventures have far outweighed the negatives, and we enjoy sharing our love of travel with our kids. We have brought them along for the ride to England, China, Peru, Jamaica, and hopefully more in the future.

The moral of the story, "Be yourself and let your kid pick out your online match for you."

Message from Lolo

The world can be a crazy place to live, but if you are looking for love but work all the time, online dating can be an excellent place to start. I have known many couples that have met online and have now been married for years. They found happiness, so it does work. Listen, if it's your time, then online dating may be the way it happens for you.

Here are a few things to be mindful of while you are on your adventure:

- Ask the question: Are you married, separated, or in a relationship. You will throw some off guard, and they will tell you the truth before they have time to think of a lie.
- Don't get caught up in words. Listen to the content.
- Do not get caught up in looks.
- Look at the heart. How do they treat others when you are together, especially servers in restaurants?
- Don't allow the word love to come too soon, especially if you are not feeling anything.
- Trust your intuition and instinct.
- If they ask you for one dime and want you to send any money via check, Western Union anything: Bye, Felicia!
- If they start talking about a family so fast that it

confuses you, pay attention. What do they really want?

- Actively listen to all conversations and remember the content.
- Remember that you are worthy of good love, and no one deserves your time if they do not reciprocate it. Pay attention if they are not actively trying to spend time with you without your prompting.
- Tell them upfront how you need to communicate with your potential mate to maintain the relationship.
- If they do not communicate with you for days at a time, pay attention. Where are you? If you are not important enough for a text ... hmmm.
- Do not lose yourself in them by changing yourself. You are awesome.
- If they are bringing more stress than happiness, it may be time to move on.
- Love yourself first, and don't seek love if you are broken from the last relationship.
- Remember, you draw to you what you are 90% of the time. My energy always brought broken men because I was broken and insecure. Now that I honor and love myself, I can spot the ones that are not for me.
- Sex is a big deal and a big question of the soul. If you are asked for sex or bodily references are made continuously, that is not love. That is a temporary need that needs to be filled for them.

- Stay true to yourself, and remember you can't be open to new love coming in if you do not love yourself first.

My true love has not found me yet, but I am open to him. I am a lot wiser than I was in 2013 when I started online dating. I have learned something from each person I have met. This is an education that no one can take from me. I am so grateful to each person who I allowed to get close to my heart, honestly. I have grown so much as a woman of peace to a woman that understands and respects the things that make me happy and honor the things that would make my new mate happy.

About the Author

Lisa J. Crawford is the CEO of LJC Motivations. She reaches thousands around the world with her message of hope, comfort, and inspiration. Lisa has more than thirty years of experience as a speaker, life coach, and author.

She holds a Business Degree in Organizational Management from Bethel University. She has been a hospitality consultant for two decades. She lives her life as a Servant Leader in every environment she enters.

Lisa was designed to help people who have experienced workplace abuse, sexual assault, and self-sabotage become their personal best. Her life experiences have allowed her to move past her pain to promote self-love and forward movement.

Lisa wants to make sure her voice and books teach the hospitality industry management how to honor and respect those who are underpaid and under-appreciated, so they know their value and worth in the workplace culture.

Contact LJ

 www.lisajcrawford.com

 ljthespeaker@gmail.com

Books by LJ Crawford

Available on Amazon

- The Master Relationship Builder Relationship Building Through the Eyes of the Employee
- Silent Screams Releasing Life's Experiences Through the Healing Power Of The Written Word
- Silent Screams Journal
- It Starts with Me
- Voices from the Edge

Available at www.lisajcrawford.com

- Speaking my Truth
- You are Enough

www.ingramcontent.com/pod-product-compliance
Lightning Source LLC
LaVergne TN
LVHW020056110826
845155LV00022B/89
* 9 7 8 1 9 4 1 7 4 9 9 8 2 *